MY PAWSOME DOG AND ME JOURNAL

Celebrate Your Dog, Map Its Milestones and Track Its Health and Well-Being

CHARLIE ELLIS

summersdale

MY PAWSOME DOG AND ME JOURNAL

Text by Kevin Woodley

An Hachette UK Company
www.hachette.co.uk

Summersdale Publishers Ltd
Part of Octopus Publishing Group Limited
Carmelite House
50 Victoria Embankment
LONDON
EC4Y 0DZ
UK

www.summersdale.com

Printed and bound in China

ISBN: 978-1-80007-419-4

Substantial discounts on bulk quantities of Summersdale books are available to corporations, professional associations and other organizations. For details contact general enquiries: telephone: +44 (0) 1243 771107 or email: enquiries@summersdale.com.

Disclaimer
None of the views or suggestions in this book is intended to replace medical opinion from a vet who is familiar with your dog's particular circumstances. If you have concerns about your dog's health, please seek professional advice.

To

From

Contents

INTRODUCTION

You never forget the first time you meet your dog. Whether you're picking up a bouncy puppy or enjoying the gentle patience of a mature dog, it won't be long before your canine companion is leaving their paw prints on your heart... and your new carpets too! But they'll make you laugh, give you cuddles when you need them, and they'll soon become a precious member of the family.

Put simply, dogs are special, and none more so than your very own whirlwind of fur and joy. This journal is for your dog. You'll have lots to learn about each other, especially toilet habits — that one is very important!

This journal is a fun way for you to keep a diary of your dog's life. Track their first mud splash, good boy (or girl) poop and slipper chewed! It's also a place for you, because owning a dog is a two-way deal, and there's lots you'll want to celebrate together!

Inside you'll find space for photos, notes and memories you won't want to forget. You'll also find advice, tips and clever tricks on how to give your dog its best life. The great part is, you can use this book to take a trip down memory lane whenever you need it, because those dog days will whizz past.

Chapter One

THE
BASICS

Taking care of a dog isn't just about going for a walk and asking them to sit. There's a whole world of canine conundrums. In this book, you'll learn all you need to know about dog breeds, settling in and even how to build your very own puppy survival kit.

Doggie Details

Owning a dog can be a bit overwhelming. You might get it wrong or forget things at first, but that's normal. Luckily, you can note down all your pup's precious details in the space provided below, so you're always prepared.

Name (pick a good one – you'll be calling it a lot):

....

Breed (because everyone will ask):

....

Birthday (don't want to forget this one – they'll be expecting a new toy):

....

Star sign (this will explain why they pulled your curtains down):

....

There is no option of no dogs on the bed.

Alicia Silverstone

Doggie Data

You've chosen your new four-legged friend, but it's more interested in the treats in your pocket than being your bestie right now. Never mind. There's still plenty you need to do before you take your perfect pooch home. First on the list is keeping a clear record of all their medical details. Use the space below to note all the important things:

Breeder contact details:...

....

Veterinary practice name/number:...

....

Vaccinations due:...

Date when it was last wormed:..

Date of last flea treatment:...

Medication (if applicable):..

Extra notes:..

....

Bringing Your Dog Home

Bringing a dog home is the most exciting moment of a dog owner's life, but you'll want to put that excitement on a lead. Everything is going to be so strange and smelly for your new poochy pal.

Make sure to have a clean space ready so your dog can explore on its own, free of anything it can chew or swallow — leaving your favourite slippers within reach is probably not a good idea! Close off any off-limit areas.

Next, let them come to you. Sitting on the floor can help make your dog feel settled quicker, but all dogs are different so be attentive and patient.

When your dog feels comfortable around you and your home, it will generally initiate play. Easy signs to look out for are wagging tails and bouncing bottoms. When your canine companion is happy and ready, it will waddle its way over to you. This is when the face licking begins and you know the fun is about to start!

WELCOME HOME CHECKLIST:

☐ Prepare a clean, open space

☐ Place valuables up high or
inside a cupboard

☐ Fill up a water and food bowl

☐ Be patient and let the dog come to you

☐ Introduce it to the toilet area
or garden if you have one

☐ Smile and grab a camera.
This is going to be amazing!

The Day We Brought You Home

Insert a photo of the day you brought your four-legged friend home in the space below:

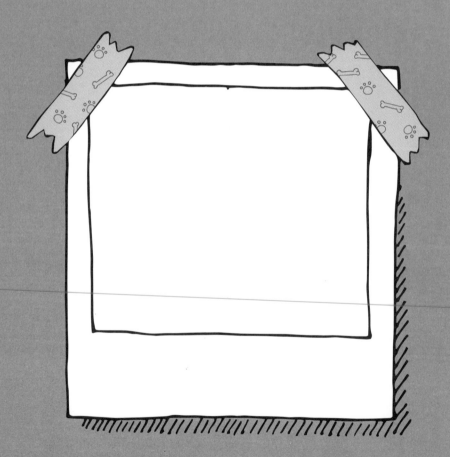

HOME IS WHEREVER YOUR DOG IS

Puppy Hacks

If you're bringing a bouncy ball of fluff (commonly called a puppy) into your home, you'll want to read these tips and tricks carefully.

- Dog clickers are helpful for positive reinforcement training and quickening the learning process. Just make sure you're not annoying anybody with it, and have treats in hand to reward your very good pup.

- Ropes are great too, especially for scratching and teething.

- Make sure you have an appropriate and fun puppy toy. You know — for the distractions.

- The biggest secret in dog ownership is a chew toy stuffed with food, keeping them full, happy and occupied for ages — and if they're happy, you'll be happy too!

- Learn to sew.

I'm suspicious of people who don't like dogs, but I trust a dog when it doesn't like a person.

Bill Murray

Survival Kit

The first few days of dog ownership can be an assault on the senses. Here's a survival guide to help you through the mayhem!

1. Biodegradable poo bags. Start practising so you're a professional poop picker.

2. Pee pads. You can put pads down to stop your dog accidentally weeing somewhere it shouldn't, but be careful they don't become too reliant.

3. A good lead. You have a choice of elastic cord or classic rope. Pick whichever you prefer, because if you're uncomfortable with your lead, your dog will end up walking you and not the other way round.

4. A crate. This is useful for training your pup to sleep on its own and gain independence. Choose one they can comfortably stand and turn around in... and howl to the moon non-stop.

5. A snug bed, sofa, or armchair of your choosing (or perhaps your own bed!). The comfiest place place in your house is now your dog's sleeping area when they're not using their crate. You might as well make peace with the idea. If your dog already owns a favourite and smelly bed, you'll want to make room for that too until they decide to commandeer the best seat in the house.

6. Dog food, toys and chew sticks.

7. A pair of comfy wellington boots for all the mud stomping and unlucky (or lucky if you would rather believe that) poo treading.

Doggie Shopping

Make a handy list of things you have
and things you still need to get:

Things we have:

_____

_____

_____

_____

_____

_____

_____

_____

_____

Need to get:

_____

_____

_____

_____

_____

_____

_____

_____

_____

AT THE
END OF A
WAGGING
TAIL IS
HAPPINESS...
AND
PROBABLY
MUD

Fantastic Facts

Dogs don't just eat, sleep and poo. Some have made a real go of it, from record-breakers to lifesavers.

RECORD HOLDERS

Purin the Beagle is the record holder for catching footballs with her front paws, managing 14 in one minute! She's the doggie keeper to beat. Something to try perhaps...

Brandy the boxer holds the award for the longest tongue at an impressive 43 cm (17 inches) — just imagine all the face licking!

Tubby the yellow Labrador rose to fame after helping his owner collect 24,000 plastic bottles on their walks together. A dog that tidies up and saves the planet? Extraordinary!

HISTORIC HEROES

Dogs are excellent cuddlers, but two in particular made history with incredible acts of bravery.

In 1925, an epidemic of diphtheria swept across the small Alaskan town of Nome. 650 miles of perilous ice separated the suffering people from the nearest supply of life-giving serum. It was Balto the Siberian husky who led the final rescue team, dragging the sleeping sled drivers to their destination and saving the day!

During World War I, a stubborn terrier called Stubby warned American soldiers of incoming bombs and gas attacks. He took out a German spy by the ankles and returned home a hero. The spirited little dog was awarded a medal for his life-saving service.

DOGGIE STARS

Plenty of dogs are quite content with sniffing their bums on the sofa, but others have become movie stars.

Toto

Terry was the dog who played the little black fluff-ball in *The Wizard of Oz* and is the inspiration to all Hollywood-dreaming Cairn terriers.

Rin Tin Tin

Rescued after World War I, Rin Tin Tin was a German shepherd who reinvented himself as a movie star in the 1920s. He starred in 26 silent films and earned a much-deserved place on the Hollywood Walk of Fame.

Lassie

You can't talk about doggie stars without mentioning Lassie, the rough collie played by a dog called Pal most notably in the iconic 1943 film *Lassie Come Home*. With kind, intelligent eyes and a nose for adventure, Lassie is a real heart-stealer.

Beethoven

A family favourite, Beethoven is the name given to the massive dog in the titular 1993 film, *Beethoven*. The dog was played by the huge and very huggable St Bernard, Chris. Between causing lots of mischief and melting hearts, the dog's popularity helped *Beethoven* win best feature film and become one of the biggest box office hits.

Who's a Good Dog? Oh, Yes You Are!

That's enough about other dogs. Let's refocus on the best pooch in the world!

What is it that you love most about your new loyal friend? Maybe your perfect pooch sings the best karaoke? Perhaps they are the best at receiving tummy rubs. Are they the laziest dog on earth or the friendliest or the smelliest or the cheekiest?

Whatever makes your dog shine above all others, write it in this box:

Group Hug

Stick a photo of you and your poochy pal here.

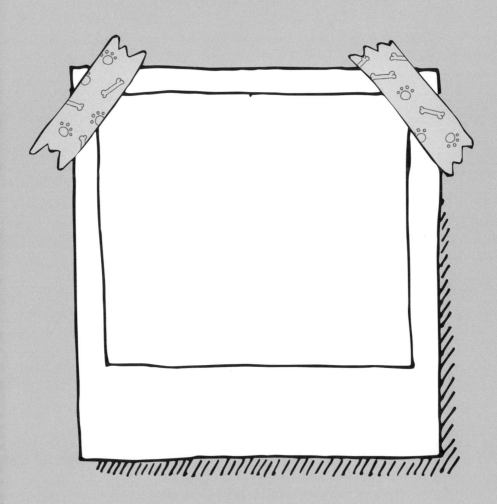

Chapter Two

DOGGIE HEALTH 101

Caring for your new dog can be overwhelming, but hopefully this chapter will take the stress out and put the fun in. Soon you'll have all the vitals covered and will know how to keep your dog in tip-top shape. Then you can get on with playing and cuddling.

My little dog —
a heartbeat
at my feet.

Edith Wharton

Setting Up Your Dog's Health

FIND A VET

Registering your tail-wagging friend with a vet should be
your top priority. Try picking one close to home. You'll
want to make travelling as easy as possible in case your
pooch whines at the very sniff of car journeys.

CONSIDER A PET PLAN

For a monthly fee you can get a range of benefits
covered, such as flea and worm treatment, nail clipping,
vaccination and health check-ups.

PET INSURANCE

Having financial cover for your doggie should they need
an important trip to the vet or long-term treatment can
help you sleep easier — and your dog snore louder.

MEDICATION

If your dog requires medication, whether from birth or due to an unfortunate development, familiarize yourself with their needs and have a dedicated doggie care box including everything your furry friend needs to be okay. Create a medication schedule to make sure everything runs smoothly too.

VACCINATIONS

Dogs can pick up all sorts of pesky diseases as they rummage about, so keep their vaccinations up to date. If unsure, ask your vet and keep a record of important dates in a safe place.

NEUTERING

No dog is going to thank you for this, but it's important to consider neutering if you wish to avoid unplanned pups, prevent illnesses and control unwanted behaviours. They'll give you sad eyes for a few days, but they'll also look completely adorable as they sulk.

Signs of Common Illnesses

DENTAL DISEASE

Symptoms include discomfort when eating, reduced appetite and weight loss. Caused by inflammation of teeth and gums, this can be treated with dental treatment and diet control.

SKIN AND FOOD ALLERGIES

Excessive scratching, diarrhoea and vomiting could indicate an allergy. This can occur with allergens that may not be new, so be attentive to any changes in your doggie's behaviour.

GASTRITIS

Characterized by prolonged vomiting, acute gastritis can resolve after 24 hours, but chronic gastritis can last up to two weeks. Your dog will have an upset stomach on the odd occasion, but extensive vomiting should be checked with a vet for safety.

Remember, if you are ever unsure, to always consult your vet.

YOUR FURRY
FRIEND WILL
STEAL YOUR
HEART;
THAT'S THE
DOGGIE DEAL

Foods You Can Share

FRUIT

Some fruits are fine for your doggie to gobble up, but you'll want to remove pips, cores or stones as these can be harmful. Bananas, apples, peaches, pears and berries are all okay, whether by accident (most likely theft) or as a treat.

VEG

Your dog can eat vegetables like celery, green beans, cooked potatoes and garden peas. They will also be excited by the thrill of leftover broccoli from your dinner plate, and a raw carrot makes a great afternoon treat.

EGGS

The sniff of a cooked egg is certain to get your doggie drooling. You better share. Eggs are nutritious too, but only in moderation as they are high in fat.

Foods You Can't

FRUIT

Some fruits will upset your curious dog. Grapes and raisins should be avoided as they are toxic and can cause vomiting and other severe complications.

ONIONS

Onions and similar foods such as garlic, chives and leeks are also toxic and not safe for your dog to eat.

MUSHROOMS

Again, mushrooms are highly toxic and should be avoided.

CHOCOLATE

Dairy found in chocolate is not good for your dog's digestion anyway, but cocoa is the main culprit here as it contains theobromine, which is very harmful to dogs.

You should always double-check with your vet before introducing new foods into your dog's diet. Dog stomachs are fussy.

(Information sourced from animaltrust.org.uk)

If I could be half
the person my
dog is, I'd be twice
the human I am.

Charles Yu

Doggie Delicious

Sharing is caring. Make a list of the food your dog munches over anything else. Your unguarded dinner counts too. They would be very disappointed if you couldn't remember.

And once you're done, make a list of all the things they would rather ignore.

My doggo's favourite munchies:.............................

....

....

....

My doggo's least favourite foods:.........................

....

....

....

Happy and Healthy

Food is fun, but there is more to keeping your dog healthy than helping them eat their way through life.

REGULAR WALKING

Exercise requirements depend on the breed, but you should aim to walk your dog at least once a day for 30 minutes to an hour.

HEALTHY WEIGHT

A healthy dog has a balance of nutrition and exercise to reduce health problems. Consult a vet for diet advice.

TEMPERATURE

Your dog should have a comfortable temperature of 38–39°C (101–102.5°F). Consider buying a dog coat in the winter and never leave your dog alone in a car or enclosed space in the summer.

CLEAN TEETH

Dogs need a good mouth scrub to avoid gum disease and stinky breath. You can use special dog toothpaste to clean their teeth — human toothpaste is not suitable. Dental sticks and chew toys can also help.

DOG WATCH

Monitoring your dog's habits is important to help recognize signs of distress early. You'll want to pay attention to any changes, such as weight loss or appetite loss as well as limping and breathing difficulties.

SHELTER

Dogs shouldn't be kept exposed to the elements for long. Plus, if they're inside you get to cuddle them.

FRESH SHEETS

Clean, dry bedding makes your dog a happy sleeper!

A HAPPY
DOG IS
ONE THAT
STRUTS

Pup-tastic Picture

It's time to show off that healthy, happy grin!
Everybody needs to see how delighted your doggo
is that you picked them over the rest.

Flea, Worm and Tick Treatments

Among the more important aspects of owning a pet is keeping them free of bothersome fleas, worms and ticks. A bit of medication and organization is all you need to protect against these tiny hijackers.

FLEAS

These miniature parasites love to live on your dog's body and suck their blood underneath all that lovely, warm fur. Beware, they will enjoy infesting your home just as much if left untreated. Signs that your dog might be suffering from fleas are excessive itching, scratching or nipping at their skin. If you're suspicious, give your dog a thorough coat inspection.

WORMS

Rather unpleasant, tapeworms are the most common worm infection for your dog. Other worms like the lungworm can be more dangerous. You'll want to look out for blood in stools, weight loss and loose droppings.

TICKS

Another pesky pest to watch out for are ticks, which attach themselves to parts of your dog's body and suck blood. Check for little bumps, especially around the head, neck, ears and feet. Remove these disease carriers quickly with spot-on treatment or tick tweezers.

Treatment

Ask your vet about setting up appropriate flea, worm and tick treatment for your dog. Effective treatments are shampoos, powders and spot-on treatments. These methods are great at killing fleas on impact and spread naturally over your dog's body. You can also use tablets; mix them with your dog's food for easy application. You should pre-emptively treat your dog for fleas once a month, and worm them once every three months.

Growing Pains

There is going to be a day when your dog becomes unwell or a doggie adventure ends in a minor disaster. Instead of letting it cloud your time together, why not reflect on it below and follow up with how things got better? Think about a challenge you and your dog got through together. Caught in a storm? Stuck down a riverbank? Lost each other in the park?

Challenge:...

How we overcame it:..

....

Notes for next time:...

....

....

Pawsome Health Plan

Make sure you've got all your doggie health bases covered with this handy checklist. The last thing you want is to forget your flea treatment and have bugs bouncing around the house.

- ☐ Vet registered
- ☐ Vaccinations scheduled
- ☐ Flea and worm treatment
- ☐ Special medication journal (if necessary)
- ☐ Neutered
- ☐ Pet plan
- ☐ Pet insurance

- ☐ Healthy dog food
- ☐ Healthy dog treats
- ☐ Healthy teeth and gums
- ☐ Perfect temperature
- ☐ Tail wagging
- ☐ Sleeping well
- ☐ Snoring loud

Chapter Three

DOGGIE MENTAL HEALTH AND WELL-BEING

Part of what allows us to love our dogs is their heartfelt range of emotional triggers, reactions and mannerisms. You might have heard about the restorative effects of a dog on its owner's mental health, but we must not forget to return the favour. It's also how the strongest bonds are formed.

A dog is a bundle of pure love, gift-wrapped in fur.

Andrea Lochen

Separation Anxiety

After leaving your dog on their own, you'll often return to find them happy to see you again. Some dogs will be more restrained, but generally, they'll show signs of affection and relief. As an owner, it's a wonderful feeling.

Sadly, this doesn't mean they haven't been distressed while you've been gone, and unless they've made a Shawshank-inspired tunnel into the neighbour's house, you might not realize anything was wrong.

With a bit of detective work you can spot the signs that indicate your dog has been unhappy when left home alone. You can then move towards creating a more relaxed environment.

Common Signs

DAMAGE

This is the clearest sign that your dog has been anxious while you've been away. It won't always be as destructive as wall damage or broken items, so look for scratch marks near doors and windows. A distressed dog left inside alone will often look for a way out.

TOILETING

You'll probably smell this one before you see it, but sometimes it can occur in otherwise safe spaces like their bedding.

NOISE

A distressed dog will whine for attention. It can be useful to ask a neighbour if they may have heard anything while you've been gone.

Leaving Your Dog Home Alone

It can be scary whenever you have to leave your doggo alone, but don't worry. There are a few ways you can help them feel more relaxed when you're not there.

BUILD CONFIDENCE

Introduce independence to your dog gradually, beginning with quick trips and gradually extending to longer journeys. The idea is to get them used to their own company. A cage in the early stages of training can also be a great way to develop your dog's confidence when you're asleep.

FOOD ALWAYS HELPS

One way to keep a dog relaxed is to keep them occupied. When alone, always leave food and water for your dog. A tasty chew treat really saves the day here.

SIMULATE COMPANY

A radio playing at a gentle volume can reduce your doggie's sense of separation anxiety.

PET CAM

Setting up a camera in your home can be a fun and informative way of monitoring your dog in secret. Some products allow you to hear your dog and communicate to them wirelessly through your phone. This can help put them at ease and will also help reveal harder to notice distress behaviours, such as pacing or salivating.

FIND A DOG-SITTER

Another option, to avoid leaving your dog for long spells on its lonesome, is to hire a dog-sitter or dog walker. Your beloved pooch gets company and exercise, and you get a free conscience!

YOU *DIDN'T*
WANT TO BE
WOKEN UP
AT 4 A.M.?
TOO BAD!

Doggie Depression

Like humans, dogs can suffer from depression. While there's no particular trigger, there are a couple of reasons that could be behind these blues.

After a significant loss of a human friend or four-legged walking buddy, dogs grieve. This can cause an unhappy demeanour and behavioural changes. Dogs also latch onto the sad feelings of humans, which only reinforces how affectionate and emotive they can be.

You should keep a lookout for other factors, like boredom. Dogs may also pick up gloomy winter moods, particularly if walks are shorter.

Dog's Got the Blues? Here's What to Do

With a little love, dogs should bounce back from depression without any professional treatment needed.

- 🐾 Remember what they enjoy and engage your dog with things that would normally bring a tail wag. It's possible that your dog just needs to dive-bomb a deep puddle.

- 🐾 Reward positive changes in their behaviour with a treat. However, don't give treats in an effort to stir your dog from their sad slumber. This will only promote a link between getting treats and feeling down.

- 🐾 Your dog needs friends too. Do it with care but get them socializing with other dogs they can cause mischief with.

Dogs are not our whole life, but they make our lives whole.

Roger Caras

Loud Bangs and Other Worries

Aside from separation anxiety, there are other doggie anxieties to watch out for. As always, the more easily you can spot triggers, the quicker you can guide your dog to being its tail-wagging, happy self.

SOCIAL ANXIETY

Not all dogs are confident. Some are a little shy. It's sweet but can be problematic when introducing them to other people or meeting other more socially adept dogs. Even in the canine kingdom you've got the loud kids and the quiet ones.

NOISE ANXIETY

Nobody likes sudden loud bangs, especially your dog with their lovely, soft ears. Be aware of any noisy disturbances that could affect your dog, such as loud music, shouting, fireworks or a crack of thunder (see page 60 for comfort tips).

COMPULSIVE BEHAVIOUR

What may appear initially as a quirky habit might actually be a sign of underlying unhealthy mannerisms your dog is developing due to stress. Typically, a sign of compulsive behaviour is a recurring habit that seems unusual, such as excessive licking or nail chewing. On the odd occasion this is perfectly fine, but in prolonged circumstances it can lead to health concerns.

Stress Signals

A lot of mental health dog signals overlap with physical concerns. If you're ever worried, consult a vet for professional advice. Owning a dog is a lot about being a good listener and dutiful watcher.

COMMON SIGNS OF STRESS:

- Loss of appetite
- Restlessness
- Social withdrawal
- Avoiding eye contact
- Excessive barking
- Sucking on toys (this one can be tricky to identify as a health worry because a lot of dogs enjoy suckling their toys)
- Chasing their tail
- Aggressive behaviour (such as snarling, barking or baring teeth)
- Excessive licking or sniffing
- Pacing
- Whining
- Trembling

THE
ONLY THING
BETTER THAN
A DOG IS
MORE DOGS

Fireworks

Exciting for people but not for your doggie, fireworks are one of the major obstacles all pet owners face and can lead to serious dog trauma and health problems.

It's a stressful time for you and your dog, but there are a few things you can do to prepare:

- In the months before common celebrations, set up a doggie safe space that's quiet and personal. You should avoid this area when your dog is exploring it so they learn that this is a space where they won't be disturbed. You can, however, train them to recognize it as a comforting place with familiar smells, toys and treats.

- Close windows and curtains. Once a dog hears that first boom in the sky, they usually won't settle until it's over — even if the sounds quieten down.

- Play the television or radio to help drown out the noise outside.

- Invest in a thundershirt. It's a pressurized vest that your dog can wear to simulate a gentle hugging sensation that promotes calming effects. Who wouldn't feel better with a constant cuddle?

- Ask your vet about medication or pheromone sprays to help relax your dog during these hectic moments.

- Do your best to soothe your dog with soft strokes.

- Talk to them. Tell them it's going to be all right.

- Notice when you need to give them space too.

Knowing Your Dog

With all the indoor and outdoor things that make your dog stressed or relaxed, it can be great to identify problem areas for your doggo and note down happy solutions.

MY DOG GETS STRESSED WHEN...

_____

_____

_____

_____

_____

_____

_____

_____

_____

_____

WHAT HELPS MY DOG RELAX IS...

Keeping Your Dog Happy

Here's a quick rundown of things that can help:

🐾 **Plenty of exercise**

A healthy body leads to a healthy mind.

🐾 **Play games that stimulate their brain, such as treasure hunt (see page 126)**

Dogs need something to keep them busy like toys, games and chew sticks.

🐾 **Refresh the toys**

Swap out their toys every few weeks to keep them interested.

🐾 **Play pup fiction or put on the radio**

That's right, you can find hours of pleasant sounds on loads of specialized apps for your doggie that will comfort them. A gentle radio is especially useful if they have to be alone for a few hours.

🐾 **Give them access to a window**

Dogs get grumpy staring at four walls. Hours of fun can be spent watching everything happening outside.

Sleepy and Happy

What does your dog look like at their most relaxed? Are they snoring? Dreaming of rabbits? Legs pointing to the sky? Perhaps they've got every single one of their toys out!

List the particular characteristics that signal to you when your dog is feeling content and relaxed:

Chapter Four

DOGGIE
COMMUNICATION

You fall in love with your doggo because of the way they communicate on a deeply emotive level. It's in their warm eyes, head nuzzles and soft paws. But since they cannot speak, it's crucial to recognize all the little signs that make up a dog's visual vocabulary.

IF YOU WAKE
UP TO FIND
YOUR DOG
SITTING ON
YOU, YOU'RE
DOING A
GOOD JOB

Being a Dog Whisperer

Understanding your dog's needs through identifying behaviours is the key to a healthy pooch and an unbreakable bond. Your dog will love you even more if you're a good doggie listener.

Observe the whole body. Dogs are always communicating, through their eyes, ears, mouth, body and tail.

Considering the context of the situation helps with the trickier aspects of doggie communication. A dog yawning when it's tired is normal. A dog yawning when it's playing might be communicating something other than tiredness or boredom.

And remember, your dog is special. Every dog, at different ages and health levels, will react differently to different situations. All you have to do is watch and learn, just like they do for you.

Dogs do speak, but only to those who know how to listen.

Orhan Pamuk

Doggie Greetings

When I'm happy to see you:

- 🐾 I'll do a big stretch down to the ground or up to your knees.
- 🐾 My ears will be relaxed.
- 🐾 My eyes will be soft and kind.
- 🐾 I might wiggle my bum and wag my tail really fast.
- 🐾 I'll pick up my toy and bring it to you.

When I'm curious or surprised:

- 🐾 I'll tilt my head to one side.
- 🐾 My tail will be raised.
- 🐾 My ears will be forward.
- 🐾 My eyes will be engaged with you.
- 🐾 I'll look cute but it just means I'm interested.

When I like a particular pooch:

- 🐾 I'll bump their nose (or dog-kiss, as we call it).
- 🐾 My eyes and ears will be soft.
- 🐾 My body will be relaxed.
- 🐾 I could be interested, content or playful.

If I smell another dog's bottom:

- 🐾 It means I'm conducting important canine-only research.
- 🐾 A quick sniff is great; we can be friends.
- 🐾 Anything longer and it might be considered rude or annoying.
- 🐾 Watch me closely and the other dog's reactions to see how our meeting is going.

Happy

When I'm happy:

- 🐾 My ears will be in a neutral state and usually soft and floppy.

- 🐾 My eyes could be soft and warm with relaxed eyelids. Sometimes I'll be squinting, which looks adorable.

- 🐾 My mouth could be relaxed with a flat tongue or one that's flopping out. I'll be smiling and yapping playfully.

- 🐾 My tail could be relaxed, high and wagging.

- 🐾 My body could be really chill. I might be leaning into you or bowing down playfully with my bottom raised.

- 🐾 My hair will be smooth and soft to stroke.

- 🐾 I'll be making excitable noises, barking in a high-pitched tone and ready for attention or play.

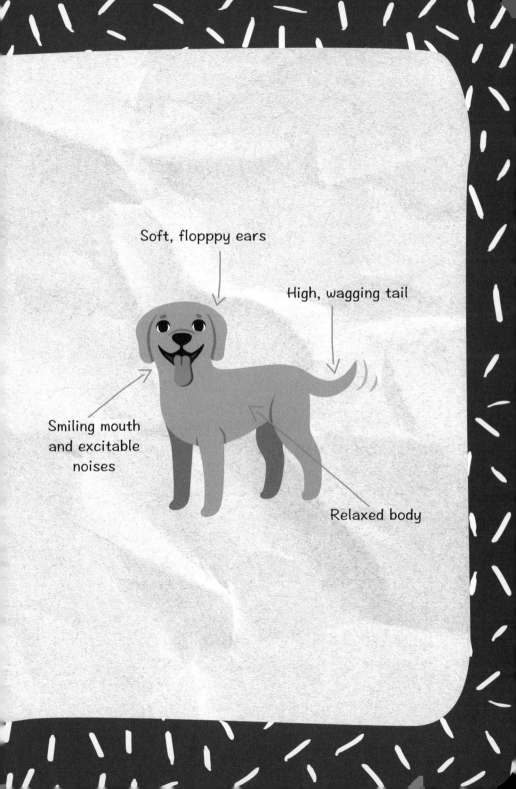

Anxious

When I'm anxious:

- 🐾 My ears could be stiff, pinned back, low and alert.

- 🐾 My eyes could be blinking or squinting a lot. I'll show the whites of my eyes, known as "whale eye" and staring in the opposite direction to where my head is facing. I might avoid eye contact.

- 🐾 I could be panting, drooling or licking my lips excessively. I could be yawning even though I'm not tired.

- 🐾 My tail could be hanging low or be tucked between my legs.

- 🐾 My body could be tense and compact. It might be turned away from you. I could be sitting or lying down to make myself smaller.

- 🐾 I might be whining, whimpering or barking excessively.

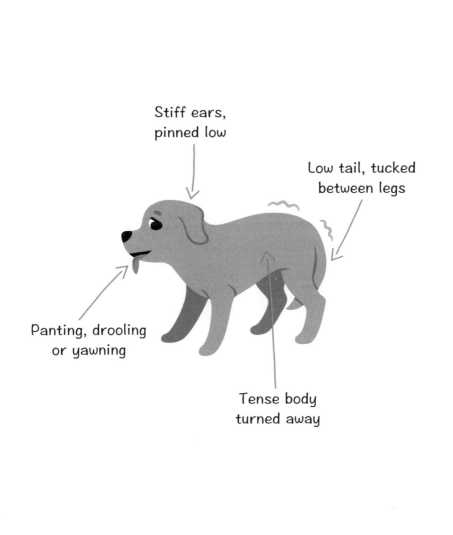

Stiff ears,
pinned low

Low tail, tucked
between legs

Panting, drooling
or yawning

Tense body
turned away

HOME IS
WHERE YOUR
HOUND IS

Wanting

When I'm wanting something:

- My body might be wiggling and my tail wagging.

- I'll be staring at you and asking questions. My eyes will be big with raised eyebrows that make me look adorable. This is commonly known as "puppy dog eyes" and if I do it for long enough, I'll probably get what I want.

- I could be barking continuously for attention.

- I could be waiting beside the door, needing to go to the toilet or having a little wander in the fresh air.

Defensive

When I'm defensive and telling you to back off:

- 🐾 My eyes might be hard, fixed and focused.
- 🐾 My ears could be high and forward.
- 🐾 My tail may be stiff and straight.
- 🐾 I might be standing with tense muscles and my body weight leaning forward.
- 🐾 I could have a wrinkled face with my teeth bared.
- 🐾 My lips could be pursed tight together or pulled back into a snarl.
- 🐾 I may bark in a loud, low-pitched tone.

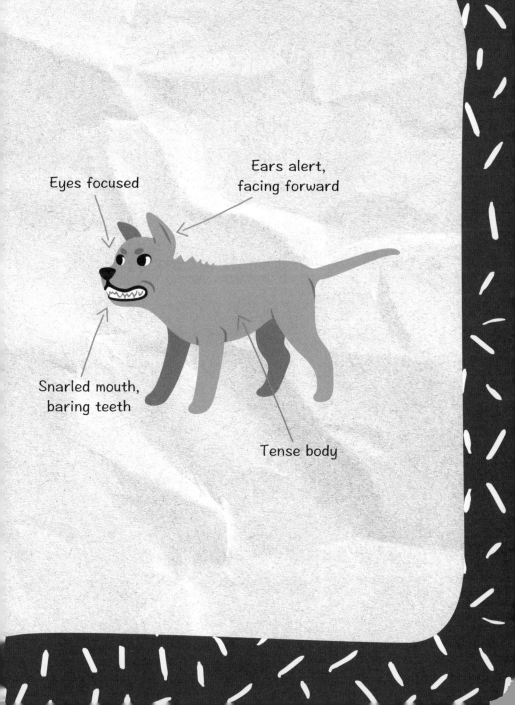

I want to work like a dog, doing what I was born to do with joy and purpose. I want to play like a dog, with total, jolly abandon.

Oprah Winfrey

Speaking My Dog's Language

Write down the signs and signals you have noticed when your dog is trying to communicate something. This will help you remember for the future, cementing your spot as a champion dog-whisperer.

Dog Talk

Test how much you've learned about doggie language with this snappy quiz. Choose one answer from the following questions. Don't stress about it, you are a canine communications expert.

Low ears pinned back means a dog is:

☐ **Anxious**

☐ **Relaxed**

☐ **Wanting**

If a dog bumps noses with another dog, it is:

☐ **Unsure**

☐ **Defensive**

☐ **Happy**

A wrinkled nose or face means a dog is:

☐ **Sad**

☐ **Happy**

☐ **Defensive**

"Whale eye" means a dog is:

- [ ] Defensive
- [ ] Anxious
- [ ] Relaxed

A dog that is defensive will be:

- [ ] Lying on their back
- [ ] Bowing down
- [ ] Leaning forwards with a rigid tail

A happy bark is:

- [ ] Deep
- [ ] Excitable with a wagging tail
- [ ] Accompanied with a tucked tail

A dog will look away if it is:

- [ ] Excited
- [ ] Hungry
- [ ] Anxious

(Find the answers on page 141.)

Chapter Five

DOGGIE GROOMING

With all the feeding, snuggling and playing, it can be easy to let grooming take a back seat. This cannot be allowed; your doggie needs to look like a professional poser for every photo opportunity. This is where a good grooming routine comes into play. With a bit of patience, this can be a great bonding activity for you both.

Pooch Perfect

While a nice pamper session will make your doggo as good-looking as ever, did you know regular grooming is beneficial for overall dog health? Whether done at home or by a professional, a regular scrub is important for removing dead skin. This reduces the chance of infection and other potential health hazards.

If you groom your dog every 4 to 6 weeks, they'll soon start to see it as a wonderful spa day rather than something scary and stressful. We all feel better after we take some time out to refresh, and your dog will be no different as it becomes calmer, more beautiful and less anxious.

Home Care

Not everyone has the finances or time to schedule a regular visit to your local grooming salon, but never fear. A well-prepared home routine can be the perfect solution. It also allows some time to bond and some silly photo opportunities.

All dogs are different. How much they enjoy a pooch pamper will vary depending on how comfortable they find home grooming. Some dogs love it, but others find it daunting and won't thank you for making them so gorgeous.

BRUSHING:

- Regular brushing keeps that wonderful hair soft and clean.

- Different brushes are required for particular hair types (see page 88), but this is a simple way of removing knots and nasties.

- Tip: brush hairier dogs outside to avoid a fluffy house.

BATHING:

- Bath time can be a heart-warming bonding moment, but some dogs can be less enthusiastic.

- Aim to wash your dog at least once a month using a dog shampoo. Human shampoo can disrupt the natural acids in your dog's skin which may make them vulnerable to parasites and viruses.

- Getting a stubborn dog into a tub can quickly turn into Bambi on ice, so if a bathtub doesn't work you can try washing them outside with a hose or bucket.

- Gently bathe your dog in warm water, ensuring you rinse off all remnants of the shampoo. Focus on their hair and body and try to keep the suds away from the ears, eyes and mouth.

Hair Care

Like people, most dogs need a regular grooming routine, even if it's only a weekly brush. This keeps their hair pristine, clean and lovely to stroke.

SHORT COAT:

Brush with a soft bristle brush to remove loose or dead hairs.

WIRE COAT:

Brush from the skin out to avoid matting using a comb or slicker brush.

LONG COAT:

Get out any tangles or matting as soon as you notice them with a pin brush.

CURLY COAT:

Brush from the skin out using a slicker brush, making sure no debris is stuck in the coat. Trim regularly to avoid matting and tangles.

DOUBLE COAT:

Regularly brush with a slicker brush to prevent undercoat hairs getting stuck in the overcoat.

Manicured Mutt

There are many options available for home nail grooming, such as scissors and clippers for smaller dogs and claw pliers for bigger dogs.

A good tip is to tire your dog out beforehand and get into the routine of massaging their paws regularly to get them used to the touch.

WHAT YOU NEED:

- A nail clipper or claw pliers
- Styptic powder
- Patience

WHAT TO DO:

1. Hold each toe firmly and slowly cut the tip from the top downwards at an angle.

2. Avoid cutting past the curve of the nail.

3. Stop when you see a circle known as the "quick", which is a doggie vein in the nail.

4. If you cut too deep, don't panic. Apply styptic powder to stem the bleeding.

Professional Care

When you don't have space or your dog is unhelpful in the grooming department, all of which is normal, a professional salon can be just the thing you both need.

Professional pet pamperers bring their experience and skills to the grooming table, making your canine companion the most dapper doggo in town.

With professional equipment and handling, they can also spot hidden issues early, such as fleas and bumps, and give your dog a thorough clean from top to bottom, including sensitive areas like eyes, ears and butt — the latter of which can be particularly untidy with hairier dogs.

You wouldn't want to make your dog unhappy at home with stressful grooming activities, which is why professional care can be a transformative option.

Matted hair, sore paws and long claws cause discomfort in dogs and can be difficult to treat at home. A groomer has the patience and experience to minimize your dog's stress when treating areas that might have gotten a little wild.

There is also the mental benefit of leaving your dog at a salon for a while. It builds independence, and socializing with other dogs is great for their mental well-being.

Happy Hearing

It's important to keep your doggo's soft and sensitive ears clean to prevent hearing problems. Check regularly for any redness, swelling, smells or wax build-up. Before you start, make sure your dog is used to you touching their ears. Ear build-up can vary between dogs, so it's best to consult your vet about the requirements for your particular pooch.

WHAT YOU NEED:

- 🐾 Cotton buds/pads
- 🐾 Vet recommended ear cleaning solution

WHAT TO DO:

1. If you're only cleaning the outside of the ear (i.e. the hairy bit!), use an ear-care solution and wipe down with cotton buds or pad.

2. To clean inside the ear canals, hold your dog's ears back and gently pour the cleaning solution into the canal. Be careful to only insert the tip of your cleaner. Massage their ears softly.

3. Never ever insert anything deep into your dog's ear canal! This can be hugely traumatic. If necessary, ask your vet for guidance.

IDENTIFYING INFECTION

Doggie ears are complex and sensitive. Due to their shape, dirt and other foreign objects can get stuck inside, particularly if your dog is an eager swimmer and river splasher. Ear cleaning can be more difficult when a deep clean is needed and they have floppy or hairy ears.

The following signs might indicate an infection:

- Dark brown or black earwax
- Funky smells coming from the ear
- Red sores
- Discharge
- Excessive ear scratching
- Shaking of the head
- Walking off balance
- Anxious or distracted eye contact

If you are worried and notice any of the common ear infection symptoms, consult a vet before cleaning the ears yourself.

Once you have had
a wonderful dog, a
life without one is
a life diminished.

Dean Koontz

Doggie Dental

Cleaning your doggo's teeth regularly can help prevent gum disease, but they won't appreciate you rummaging around inside their mouth. Before the brush comes out, it's best to build up a routine of massaging their lips with your fingers to get them more comfortable.

WHAT YOU NEED:

- Doggie toothpaste — not regular toothpaste
- Dog-specific toothbrush or finger brush
- Patience

WHAT TO DO:

1. Massage their lips with your finger in a circular motion for 1 minute. Practise this regularly, then repeat with their teeth.

2. Test the toothpaste on their lips to see how your dog feels about healthy gums and fresh breath. Hopefully, you will have discovered they have a passion for dental hygiene.

3. Introduce the brush! Move the toothbrush across their lips in a circular motion.

4. Lift your dog's lips and gently clean their teeth with the toothpaste in circular motions, focusing on removing tartar.

Splendid Sight

Keeping your dog's eyes clean is necessary to prevent infections, but it's a sensitive area and so requires a little extra care. Keep an eye out for signs of infections such as discharge, trouble opening eyes, uneven sizes, cloudiness and rubbing them often.

WHAT YOU NEED:

- A damp cotton ball or soft cloth

WHAT TO DO:

1. Make sure the area is well lit.
2. Check that your dog's eyes are clear and equally sized.
3. Pull down their lower eyelids to inspect the lining — it should be pink.
4. Gently wipe outward with a damp cloth, removing gunk or dirt.
5. Take it slow and be careful to avoid poking or scratching their eyeball.

COMMON EYE PROBLEMS:

- 🐾 Cataracts: cloudiness of the pupil and unsure movement due to impaired vision

- 🐾 Conjunctivitis: red, swollen eyes with discharge

- 🐾 Glaucoma: pressure behind the eye causes it to enlarge, turning the cornea cloudy

- 🐾 Progressive Retinal Atrophy: a serious condition indicated by dilated pupils and night-time blindness that worsens over time

If you notice something unusual about your dog's eyes, take them to the vet as soon as possible to prevent further damage. Protect their eyes in day-to-day activities through regular checks, trimming around the eyes in long-haired dogs and not letting them lean their head out of moving car windows, no matter how much joy it brings you both!

COMING HOME
TO YOUR DOG
WILL ALWAYS
MAKE YOUR DAY
BETTER

You do not own a dog. You have a dog. And the dog has you.

Chelsea Handler

Before the Groom

Stick in a photo of your messy, hairy dog so they never forget how scraggy they were.

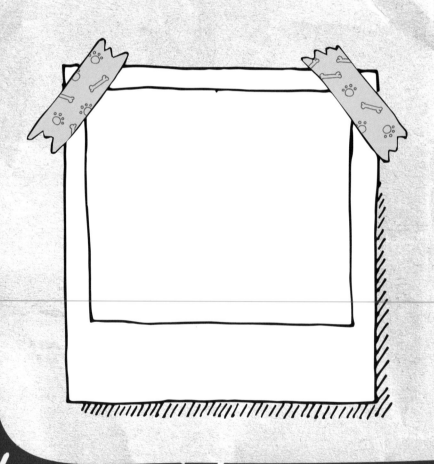

After the Groom

Show off how tremendous your doggo looks after a good scrub and brush. And to commemorate the occasion, stick in an old tuft of doggie hair saved from the groom.

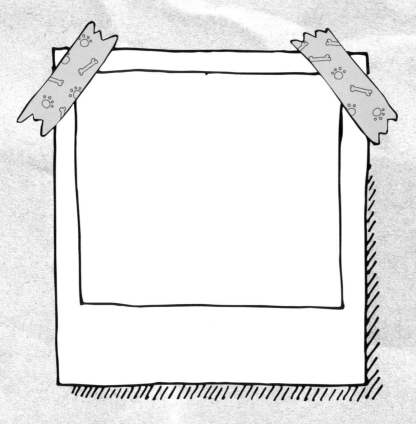

Best Grooming Techniques

Keep track of the grooming methods that work well for your dog so you don't forget! This way you'll always have the best-looking pooch in town.

The nail clippers that work best...

The best type of brush...

The perfect shampoo..

The best ear care solution...

The best place to wash my dog..

The best grooming salon...

Contact details of our favourite groomer..

....

PERMANENT
HAPPINESS IS
PAWSSIBLE,
BUT ONLY
WITH A
PUPPY

Chapter Six

DOGGIE TRAINING

Training your dog sounds like the least enjoyable part of your time together, but this simply isn't the case. Training provides intimacy, lots of laughs and it won't just be your dog learning a trick or two, you'll be learning lots about how best to interact with your dog too. It is important to train your dog so that they can remain calm when left alone and respond safely to you and others.

A well-trained dog will make no attempt to share your lunch. He will just make you feel so guilty that you cannot enjoy it.

Helen Thomson

All Aboard the Dog Train

There are different types of dog training, each with its benefits. Your dog may respond to one better than the other, so change it up if something isn't working.

POSITIVE REINFORCEMENT

The most common way to train a dog. It works through a routine of teaching your dog to perform commands, praising them, then rewarding with a treat. They associate good behaviour with tasty benefits, meaning they'll want to listen to you more.

CLICKER

Like positive reinforcement, clickers are used to show a dog they have achieved the desired result. For example: your dog sits, you click. Because they are instantaneous, clickers are a very effective training method.

SCIENTIFIC

Based on behavioural science, this training method requires research into dog psychology. Trainers teach by communicating with the dog in ways they comprehend. It can include positive and negative reinforcement and teaching by example, among other methods. It can be an illuminating, successful way to train, but is better suited to professional trainers.

MIRROR TRAINING

This method works on the principle that dogs learn through observation. By using a dog or person to perform the desired task, your dog watches and mimics the set behaviour.

Sit!

Sit! It snaps right off the tongue, as satisfying as commands go. But if your dog isn't properly trained, it only leads to red-faced embarrassment and a puzzled-looking, head-tilting dog. Fortunately, it's one of the best places to begin your dog training.

Remember, dogs happily take edible bribes.

1. Get your dog in a standing position. Hold a treat in front of their nose. If they eat it, it's an unfortunate start!

2. With the treat, move your hand over their head. Hopefully, in their attempt to follow the food with their head, your dog's bottom will have touched the floor.

3. As soon as they sit, praise and reward with the treat.

4. Once you've practised this, add "sit" as their bottom touches the ground.

5. Repeat regularly in short bursts.

Fill in a gold star each time your doggie sits like a good boy or girl. Once they hit ten, treat yourself instead (dog biscuits are not recommended).

Lie Down

Once your dog has mastered sitting, it's time to get them lying down without a fuss. This is useful for when you need more control in busier or public environments.

1. Hold a treat to your dog's nose. Move your hand with the treat down their chest and to the floor.

2. Your dog should follow the food, putting them into a lying down position.

3. Say "lie down!" when your dog drops to the floor.

4. Praise, reward and repeat.

LOVE IS
FEELING THE
SNUGGLE
OF A
WARM PUPPY

Stay!

Sometimes you just want to keep your dog still, for discipline as well as safety. It keeps them calm and smart when crossing roads and meeting new people and other dogs. It can be used for a variety of playful situations too.

1. At home, tell your dog to sit and give them a treat when they do, then ask them to get back up.

2. Tell them sit again but wait a few seconds before rewarding them when they sit down.Repeat and mix up the length of delay times between sitting and rewarding.

3. The next time they sit like a good dog, raise your hand with your palm facing outwards and tell them to "stay". Only say it once. Move away a couple of steps. If they stay, give them a treat.

4. Increase distances and change environments or rooms.

5. When comfortable, take your training outside to a park or field. Tell your dog to "stay" and move away to a challenging distance. If your dog hasn't moved, walk back to them, then praise and reward. If they get too excited or worried and don't stay, reduce your distances and try again, and increase gradually.

Recall

There's nothing more awkward than yelling helplessly during a walk, only for that cheeky pooch to nonchalantly turn away and stick their tail in the air. It will happen, so don't worry. Keep practising until that wonderful moment clicks and they come charging back.

1. At home, have your treat ready in hand so that your dog can see it.

2. Move away from your dog. A friend or partner can help by holding on to the dog's collar while you make some distance.

3. Get down low with the treat. Call your dog in an encouraging, clear voice.

4. When your dog hurtles towards you, reward with a treat. It's important not to scold your dog as this will confuse them. When they come to you, only respond positively, even if takes a while.

5. Increase distances and vary locations, such as the garden or different rooms in the house.

6. Once comfortable, move the training to an outside public area. You can keep your dog on an extendable lead until you feel confident in letting them wander freely.

Professional Dog Training

It can be lovely to train your doggo at home but there's no guarantee they'll always respond effectively. Professional dog training or dog schools are safe spaces where you can learn in a tailored environment with a qualified dog trainer, as well as other owners and their dogs, making it great for socializing too.

A FEW THINGS DOG SCHOOLS INCLUDE:

- A network of professional trainers
- Physical and virtual classes
- Walking your dog on a lead
- Socializing appropriately with other dogs
- Toilet training
- Recall training
- Understanding doggie behaviour and signals
- Building a strong bond with your dog

WHAT TO LOOK FOR IN A DOG SCHOOL:

1. A controlled atmosphere. Lots of noise indicates a chaotic learning environment that is not useful for you or your dog.

2. Positive reward-based training. This training method is effective, safe and generates happiness.

3. Small class size. Anything more than eight dogs could result in a stressful environment and not enough attention paid to your pooch.

4. Doggie behaviour. The other dogs should be relaxed and engaged and not afraid or anxious.

5. Flexible environment. Every dog responds in its own way. A good dog trainer caters to all dog types, interests and ability levels.

Dogs and angels are
not very far apart.

Charles Bukowski

Toilet Training

Whether you have a puppy or an older dog that needs reminding, toilet training is essential.

THE NEED-TO-GO SIGNS:

- Moving in a circle
- Persistent fidgeting
- Sniffing around (for the elusive perfect spot)

WHAT TO DO:

1. Get into a routine of letting your dog outside each morning.

2. In all cases, when you think they need the toilet, show your dog the correct space. You can also let them outside routinely and see if they go to the toilet.

3. If they try to go in the wrong place, guide your dog to the designated area instead of telling them off.

4. Pick a command such as "go pee" or "quickly" so they associate it with their smelly doggie business.

5. Reward and praise every time they've been to the toilet in the right place.

Trainer's Checklist

Keep track of your dog's training. Once they've mastered basic doggie training, make sure to give them a big, tasty reward.

- ☐ Sit (a good dog)
- ☐ Lie down (a really good dog)
- ☐ Stay (still as a statue)
- ☐ Recall (comes back like a boomerang)
- ☐ Toilet (we're a team: proper pooper and pooper scooper!)

DAYS WITHOUT INCIDENT

On the page opposite, fill in a square for each day your dog doesn't make a toilet mess inside. If they break the chain, go back to the first spot and begin again. When you make it to ten consecutive days, you can pat yourself on the back; your dog is a master pooper. Give them a big treat!

TOILET TRAINED

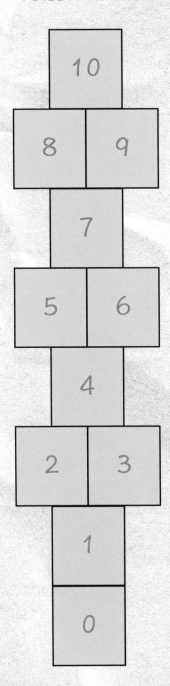

Chapter Seven

DOGGIE ACTIVITIES

Once you've mastered basic training, you and your dog are ready to move on to something more challenging, why not give these activities a try? Your dog should be well equipped to handle a variety of engaging, entertaining games that exercise both their mind and senses. These are fun activities, easy to learn and implement into your routine, and a fantastic way to bond with your dog, developing their doggie instincts at the same time.

My fashion philosophy is, if you're not covered in dog hair, your life is empty.

Elayne Boosler

Hide and Seek

Hide and seek is as classic as games come but is still one of the best and easiest games you can play with your doggo. Perfect for rainy days, and better still, it's completely free.

WHAT YOU NEED:

- Just you and your excited doggie — and treats — which, if you're reading this book, you should have...

HOW TO PLAY:

1. Once your dog has mastered sit, stay and recall, hide and seek will come naturally to them and should be simple to teach. Choose a starting room and lead your doggie there.

2. Tell your doggie to sit and stay. Smile lots, this is fun!

3. Hide yourself in a different room. Giggle if you want.

4. Call your doggie in a clear, excitable voice.

5. Rejoice as they find you easily because dogs are smart and very good at hide and seek.

6. Reward them with plenty of praise, treats and a good head ruffle.

7. If you've developed a good trust with your dog you can take this outside for a more challenging game. Just make sure to have an answer ready if somebody spots you hiding behind a tree!

Treasure Hunt

Treasure hunt is similar to hide and seek, but this time you're hiding treats around the house for your doggie to find and wolf down. It's a great game for engaging their brain and their incredible sense of smell.

WHAT YOU NEED:

- A handful of small treats

HOW TO PLAY:

1. Tell your dog to stay and show them the treats.
2. Scatter them nearby so your dog can see.
3. Tell your dog to "go".
4. Once familiar with the routine, hide the treats in different places.
5. Say "go" and watch your dog scamper away with joy.
6. Praise them when they find all the treats.

PITY THE
OWNER WHO
LOSES THE
DOG BALL

Muffin Tray Puzzle

This is another game fantastic for making your dog happy and smart. It doesn't require too much, can be done at home and can made by anyone.

WHAT YOU NEED:

- ✺ Muffin tray
- ✺ Tennis balls (or other items similar in size that fit the tray holes)
- ✺ Treats

HOW TO PLAY:

1. Fill the muffin cups with treats and let your dog scoop them out. This will show your dog that this is a place where they can find treats.

2. Refill the cups with treats then cover them with the tennis balls. This time, your dog will have to move the balls out of the way to get their reward.

3. Repeat this a few times to build up a routine.

4. Next, leave some muffin cups empty of treats, but remember to cover the empty spots with tennis balls. The more balls you have, the more complicated the game for your dog, and the more they have to engage their hunting instincts.

5. This game will teach them perseverance and deduction abilities as they sniff out their tasty treats.

Smelly Shoebox

Another easy homemade activity for your doggie requires keeping your shoeboxes instead of throwing them away.

WHAT YOU NEED:
- 🐾 Shoebox
- 🐾 Treats

HOW TO PLAY:

1. Fill a shoebox with treats. If your box is lidless, turn it upside down.

2. Put it somewhere in the room and tell your dog to find the treats. You can make it easier for your dog by poking holes in the box.

3. Increase difficulty by adding more boxes, leaving some empty.

4. Spread them around the house to make it a challenge for your dog to identify the correct boxes.

Tug of War

Food games are fun, but what if you want something a bit more invigorating? Tug of war can appear a little rough, but it's great for keeping your dog's teeth strong.

WHAT YOU NEED:
- 🐾 Dog rope

HOW TO PLAY:
1. Hold one end of the rope and draw your dog's attention to the other. If they're in a playful mood, they should catch on easily.

2. Pull gently to test your dog's behaviour. If they're keen, they'll tug back.

3. Tug back and forth. Be careful not to let your dog be too aggressive.

4. Let your dog win sometimes!

Tug of War Scoreboard

Having fun playing tug of war? Keep
a score of who's winning!

Me	My doggo
_____	_____
_____	_____
_____	_____
_____	_____
_____	_____
_____	_____
_____	_____
_____	_____

If your dog doesn't
like someone,
you probably
shouldn't either.

Jack Canfield

Which Hand Game

Sometimes you just want to keep things sweet and simple. With a little dedication, you can turn this hungry activity into an effective training exercise. This can be a little trickier for your dog to learn, so don't worry if they don't catch on straight away.

WHAT YOU NEED:
- 🐾 Treats

HOW TO PLAY:
1. Get your doggie's favourite treats and tell them to sit.
2. Let your dog see which hand you hide the treats in.
3. Hide your hands behind your back and switch the treats.
4. Put both hands out in closed fists and ask your dog which hand.
5. If they paw or nose-bump the correct hand, give them the treat and praise.

Cup Game

This home-made doggie detective game is a less messy option than using old shoeboxes! Simply grab cups of any size; yogurt pots are ideal. Make sure they are well cleaned out.

WHAT YOU NEED:

- Clean, empty pots
- Treats

HOW TO PLAY:

1. Take three cups and fill one of them with treats.

2. Ask your dog to sit, then turn the cups face-down, lifting the one containing treats so that your dog can see them. Place the cup back over the treats.

3. Shuffle the cups.

4. Ask your doggie to find the treats.

5. You could make it harder by adding more cups and filling more than one with treats.

Treat-Filled Toy

Dog owners swear by their treat-filled toys, and for good reason too: they keep your dog occupied, entertained and fed! They are the best thing to leave your doggo with whenever you need to leave them home alone, but you should test them out first with supervision.

WHAT YOU NEED:
- Treat-fillable toy
- Treats

HOW TO PLAY:
1. Take the treat-fillable toy and stuff it with your dog's favourite food.
2. Put it down and let your dog get on with it. Treat-filled toys are designed to make it easy for your dog to tackle but challenging enough to stimulate their hungry doggie brains. You can use treat dispensers instead of a toy if you wish.

NO MATTER
WHAT ANYBODY
SAYS, ROLLING
ON THE FLOOR
WITH YOUR
DOG IS MORE
IMPORTANT

Doggie Adventures

Plenty of home games can make your dog happy but none will excite your dog like a good mud tumble outside. How many of the goals below can you complete together (maybe not the icky ones)?

Check them off as you go!

- [ ] Walked the same route in all four seasons
- [ ] Stayed away from home together (camping or in a dog-friendly hotel)
- [ ] Climbed a hill
- [ ] Went to the beach
- [ ] Explored a forest
- [ ] Went on a double-date with another dog walker and their doggie friend
- [ ] Introduced ourselves to the neighbours
- [ ] Had a picnic
- [ ] Made a new friend
- [ ] Met up with an old friend
- [ ] Saw a squirrel or rabbit for the first time
- [ ] Chased a butterfly
- [ ] Dived into a bush
- [ ] Rolled in poo (ew!)
- [ ] Had a good wash at home
- [ ] Walked without a lead

My Dog's Favourite Activities

Which activities are your dog's favourites? Rate them below so you always know how to cheer your dog up.

	Enjoyment	Ability
Hide and Seek	🐾🐾🐾🐾🐾	🐾🐾🐾🐾🐾
Treasure Hunt	🐾🐾🐾🐾🐾	🐾🐾🐾🐾🐾
Muffin Tray Puzzle	🐾🐾🐾🐾🐾	🐾🐾🐾🐾🐾
Smelly Shoebox	🐾🐾🐾🐾🐾	🐾🐾🐾🐾🐾
Tug of War	🐾🐾🐾🐾🐾	🐾🐾🐾🐾🐾
Which Hand Game	🐾🐾🐾🐾🐾	🐾🐾🐾🐾🐾
Cup Game	🐾🐾🐾🐾🐾	🐾🐾🐾🐾🐾
Treat-Filled Toy	🐾🐾🐾🐾🐾	🐾🐾🐾🐾🐾
Beach Trip	🐾🐾🐾🐾🐾	🐾🐾🐾🐾🐾
Forest Trek	🐾🐾🐾🐾🐾	🐾🐾🐾🐾🐾
Meeting Four-Legged Friends	🐾🐾🐾🐾🐾	🐾🐾🐾🐾🐾
Rolling in All Kinds of Poop	🐾🐾🐾🐾🐾	🐾🐾🐾🐾🐾

CONCLUSION

Sadly, just like that, this book has come to an end. And if there's one thing to take away with you, it's that those first special weeks with your pawsome dog are going to slip into memory just as quickly. So enjoy them, cherish them, create lots of wonderful moments and keep them somewhere safe.

Hopefully, this doggie journal has inspired you to make your own book of woofs and waddles, for all the years you have left together, and all the excitement and snuggles to come.

This book is about welcoming your dog into your life, being prepared for what might come up and what adventures you can have along the way. It's also about what it means to be a dog owner, for you and for the doggo, and about the promise you make when you bring a four-legged friend home. Take care of each other and share the food.

Quiz Answers

Low ears pinned back means a dog is: Anxious

If a dog bumps nose with another dog, it is: Happy

A wrinkled nose or face means a dog is: Defensive

"Whale eye" means a dog is: Anxious

A dog that is defensive will be: Leaning
forward with a rigid tail

A happy bark is: Excitable with a wagging tail

A dog will look away if it is: Anxious

Image credits

pp.1, 3, 6-7, 8, 10, 14, 16, 17, 25, 27, 28, 29, 32, 36, 41, 44, 46, 47, 54, 55, 65, 66, 68, 69, 80, 84, 89, 94, 99, 100, 101, 104, 105, 110, 118, 122, 123, 126, 132, 133, 136, 140-141 — bone and paw icons © Viktoria Kurpas/Shutterstock.com; pp.4-5, 12-13, 18-19, 22-23, 24-25, 30-31, 34-35, 38-39, 42-43, 48-49, 50-51, 56-57, 60-61, 62-63, 70-71, 72-73, 74-75, 78-79, 82-83, 86-87, 90-91, 92-93, 96-97, 100-101, 106-107, 108-109, 112-113, 114-115, 116-117, 124-125, 128-129 — background pattern © rinrin_gs/Shutterstock.com; pp.6, 53, 140 — dog faces © TWINS DESIGN STUDIO/Shutterstock.com; pp.7, 9, 13, 23, 31, 37, 39, 44, 48, 65, 81, 85, 141 — dogs © Bibadash/Shutterstock.com; pp.9, 12-13, 16, 20, 22-23, 26, 30-31, 32, 37, 38-39, 44, 45, 48-49, 54, 56-57, 58, 62-63, 65, 68, 72-73, 78-79, 81, 85, 86-87, 89, 92-93, 95, 100-101, 108-109, 110, 114-115, 119, 120, 121, 124-125, 126, 130, 132, 134, 136, 138, 139 — paper texture © Paladin12/Shutterstock.com; pp.10, 17, 29, 36, 47, 55, 69, 80, 94, 99, 105, 118, 123, 133 — paint effect © Marish/Shutterstock.com; pp.14, 27, 41, 100, 101 — photo frame © sinoptic/Shutterstock.com; pp.15, 21, 33, 40, 52, 59, 67, 76, 98, 103, 111, 127, 137 — dog icons © ZHUKO/Shutterstock.com; p.16 — dog © TWINS DESIGN STUDIO/Shutterstock.com; p.16 — dog accessories © Amalga/Shutterstock.com; pp.19, 25, 144 — dogs © TWINS DESIGN STUDIO/Shutterstock.com; p.20 — dog accessories © Polina Tomtosova/Shutterstock.com; p.26 — frame © ricorico/Shutterstock.com; p.32, 43, 51 — dogs © TWINS DESIGN STUDIO/Shutterstock.com; pp.60-61 — fireworks © dumuluma/Shutterstock.com; pp.63, 73, 75, 77, 79 — dogs © Sudowoodo/Shutterstock.com; pp.86-87 — grooming icons © Natasha Pankina/Shutterstock.com; p.91 — dog in towel © Polina Yanchuk/Shutterstock.com; p.107 — dog icons © SunshineVector/Shutterstock.com

Have you enjoyed this book?
If so, find us on Facebook at
Summersdale Publishers, on Twitter
at @Summersdale and on Instagram
at @summersdalebooks and get in touch.
We'd love to hear from you!

www.summersdale.com